LLM FOR DATA SCIENTISTS AND ANALYSTS

A Practical Guide to Shaping the Future with Language Models for Tech Enthusiasts

Written By

Chris C. Thompson

Table of Contents

INTRODUCTION

UNLEASH THE POWER OF LANGUAGE: WELCOME TO YOUR LLM DATA SCIENCE ADVENTURE!

Imagine a world where data speaks back, revealing hidden patterns and unlocking profound insights buried deep within text. This isn't science fiction; it's the exciting reality fueled by Large Language Models (LLMs), and you hold the key to unlocking its potential.

This book is your passport to this thrilling data science revolution. Whether you're a seasoned analyst yearning to push the boundaries of your craft or a tech-savvy enthusiast eager to explore the cutting edge, this guide will equip you with the knowledge and tools to wield the power of LLMs like a pro.

But wait, hold on to your hard drives! This isn't some dry, academic tome filled with jargon and cryptic formulas. We're ditching the intimidation factor and diving headfirst into the world of LLMs with a conversational flair. Think of it as an engaging dialogue with a friendly data science mentor, one who's here to break down complex concepts into bite-sized, actionable steps.

So, buckle up and get ready to:

- **Demystify the LLM hype:** We'll separate the fact from the fiction, stripping away the buzzwords and unveiling the true potential of these language transformers.
- **Master the fundamentals:** Get a rock-solid grasp of how LLMs work, from their inner workings to their impact on the data science landscape.
- **Get hands-on:** No more theory! Dive into practical tutorials and real-world examples, learning how to leverage LLMs for tasks like sentiment analysis, text classification, and even building chatbots.
- **Explore the future:** We'll peek beyond the horizon, showcasing cutting-edge advancements and emerging trends in the LLM world.
- **Shape your career:** Discover how LLMs are transforming the data science job market and equip yourself with the skills to thrive in this dynamic field.

But that's just a taste of the adventure that awaits. Are you ready to unlock the secrets of text data, generate creative content with the power of AI, and become a pioneer in the LLM revolution? Turn the page, and let's embark on this exciting journey together! Remember, the future of data science is written in code, and with this book, you hold the pen.

PART 1: DEMYSTIFYING LLMS AND THEIR DATA SCIENCE IMPACT

CHAPTER 1

WELCOME TO THE LANGUAGE MODEL REVOLUTION: WHERE DATA LEARNS TO TALK BACK

Welcome aboard, fellow data explorers! Buckle up, because we're about to embark on a thrilling voyage into the world of Large Language Models (LLMs). Forget dry textbooks and intimidating formulas – this is an adventure powered by curiosity, practical insights, and, yes, a healthy dose of fun.

1.1 What are LLMs and Why Should You Care?

Large Language Models (LLMs): Your Text Analysis Powerhouse

Imagine analyzing mountains of text data, from customer reviews to research papers, and effortlessly extracting key insights or crafting new content. That's the power of LLMs, advanced AI models trained on massive text datasets. Think of them as super-analysts, understanding and manipulating language with exceptional fluency.

Why are LLMs becoming must-have tools for data scientists and beyond?

- o **Unlock hidden patterns:** Instead of manually sifting through text, LLMs can analyze millions of reviews to identify common themes, positive/negative sentiment, or emerging trends. Imagine understanding what truly resonates with your customers or predicting future demand through social media analysis – all thanks to LLMs.
- o **Predict future events:** By analyzing news articles and financial reports, LLMs can identify subtle shifts in language that might signal upcoming market changes or customer sentiment fluctuations. They can even analyze historical data to forecast future product trends or potential risks.
- o **Automate tasks:** Gone are the days of manually summarizing lengthy reports or translating documents. LLMs can automatically generate concise summaries of complex texts, saving you valuable time and effort. Plus, they can translate languages with impressive accuracy, breaking down communication barriers and opening up global markets.

Hold on, LLMs aren't magic wands... yet:

- **They're still learning:** Like any student, LLMs can make mistakes. Biases in their training data can lead to skewed results, and understanding sarcasm or irony can be a challenge. It's crucial to use them responsibly and be aware of their limitations.
- **Continuous improvement:** Research is constantly pushing the boundaries of LLMs, making them more accurate, fair, and versatile. By using them ethically and responsibly, we can contribute to their positive development.

Ready to see LLMs in action? Here's a simple example:

Imagine you have a dataset of customer reviews for your product. You want to understand what customers like and dislike. An LLM can analyze the text and find recurring keywords or phrases associated with positive and negative sentiment.

Here's a snippet of Python code using the Hugging Face library to achieve this:

```python
Python
from transformers import pipeline

# Load the sentiment analysis pipeline
sentiment_analysis                              =
pipeline("sentiment-analysis")
```

```
# Sample customer reviews
reviews = ["This product is amazing! Love
the features.", "Disappointed with the
quality. Didn't meet expectations."]

# Analyze sentiment
for review in reviews:
    result = sentiment_analysis(review)
    print(f"{review}: {result['label']}")
```

This code outputs the sentiment (positive or negative) for each review.

LLMs are more than just fancy buzzwords. They're powerful tools with real-world applications. As they continue to evolve, their potential to transform data analysis, communication, and even content creation is vast. Stay tuned to explore more practical examples and delve deeper into the exciting world of LLMs!

1.2 LLM Hype vs. Reality: Separating Fact from Fiction

Picture this: You hear about AI models reading millions of texts and writing like humans. "Amazing!" you think, "Can it finally write my marketing copy and analyze customer reviews?" Hold on! Let's separate the LLM hype from reality.

Hype:

Superhuman Text Masters: Imagine LLMs understanding every sentence perfectly, generating flawless creative content, and predicting trends with ease. Sounds too good to be true, right?

Data Science Revolution: Headlines claim LLMs will solve all your data analysis woes, uncovering hidden gems and automating everything. But can they wirklich (German for "really") do it all?

AI Magic Wand: Some portray LLMs as a universal fix, instantly solving complex problems with no effort. Remember, even magic wands need skilled users!

Reality:

Learning is Key: LLMs are impressive, but they're still young learners. Biases in their training data can lead to skewed results, and sarcasm or irony might fly over their heads. Think of them as brilliant students, still needing guidance.

Not a One-Size-Fits-All Fix: While LLMs have superpowers, they can't solve every data problem. They need careful integration with your specific task, data understanding, and constant monitoring. It's like using the right tool for the job – a hammer won't fix your leaky faucet.

Responsible Use Matters: Like any powerful tool, LLMs can be misused. Understanding their limitations and using them ethically is crucial to avoid spreading misinformation or causing harm. Remember, with great power comes great responsibility!

But don't ditch LLMs just yet!

Real Potential: They can automate tasks like summarizing text, translating languages, and even writing basic reports, saving you valuable time and effort. Imagine an LLM summarizing customer reviews or translating marketing materials – pretty handy, right?

Constant Evolution: Researchers are constantly improving LLMs, making them more accurate, fair, and versatile. Think of it as ongoing training – they're getting better every day!

Exciting Opportunities: With responsible development and use, LLMs have the potential to revolutionize fields like data science, communication, and even education. Just imagine personalized learning powered by LLMs!

Remember:

LLMs are powerful tools, but they're not perfect.
Use them responsibly and understand their limits.
The future of LLMs is bright, with exciting possibilities across many fields.

Now, for some real examples:

- **Analyzing Customer Reviews:** You have 10,000 reviews. Can an LLM help? Yes! Here's a Python code snippet using Hugging Face:

```python
Python
from transformers import pipeline

sentiment_analysis                    = pipeline("sentiment-analysis")

reviews   =   ["Love   this   product!", "Disappointed with customer service."]

for review in reviews:
    result = sentiment_analysis(review)
    print(f"{review}: {result['label']}")
```

This code analyzes sentiment, helping you understand overall customer satisfaction.

Generating Creative Text: Need basic product descriptions? Here's another code example:

```Python
from transformers import pipeline

text_generation                              =
pipeline("text-generation")

prompt = "Write a short description for a
new phone"

result = text_generation(prompt)
print(result[0]['generated_text'])
```

This code gives you a starting point for your description, but remember, human creativity is still irreplaceable!
LLMs are a powerful force in the tech world, but understanding their hype and reality is key to using them effectively and responsibly. Stay tuned for more exploration of their potential and limitations!

1.3 LLMs: Transforming the Data Science Landscape

Remember those mountains of text data gathering dust in your servers? LLMs (Large Language Models) are like supercharged miners, extracting valuable insights and automating tasks, transforming the data science landscape. Let's explore their current applications and future potential, with some real-world examples and even code snippets!

Current Applications:

- **Customer Whisperers:** Unravel the mysteries of customer feedback. Imagine analyzing thousands of reviews to understand overall sentiment, identify common themes, and even predict future trends. Here's a Python code snippet using Hugging Face:

Python
```python
from transformers import pipeline

sentiment_analysis = pipeline("sentiment-analysis")

reviews = ["Fantastic product! Best purchase ever!", "Disappointed with quality. Doesn't work as advertised."]

for review in reviews:
    result = sentiment_analysis(review)
    print(f"{review}: {result['label']}")
```

This code classifies sentiment as positive or negative, giving you a quick gauge of customer satisfaction.

- **Taming Textual Beasts:** No more drowning in lengthy reports or struggling with foreign languages. LLMs can automatically summarize complex documents, translate them seamlessly, and even answer specific questions buried within the text. Imagine instantly understanding key points from research papers or effortlessly communicating with international partners.

- **Future Foreseers:** Gain a glimpse into tomorrow's trends. By analyzing vast amounts of news articles, financial reports, or social media data, LLMs can predict market shifts, identify potential customer sentiment fluctuations, or even warn of upcoming risks. Think of it as having a crystal ball powered by text analysis!

Future Potential:

- **Content Creation Powerhouse:** Generate personalized marketing copy, product descriptions, or even blog posts tailored to specific audiences. Imagine creating targeted and engaging content without spending hours writing yourself. LLMs could revolutionize content creation, saving time and resources.
- **Hidden Pattern Hunters:** Go beyond the surface and uncover hidden gems in your data. LLMs can analyze vast amounts of text, identifying subtle patterns and relationships that traditional methods might miss. Imagine discovering groundbreaking insights in scientific research, social trends, or even historical documents, leading to exciting breakthroughs.

- **Data for Everyone:** Democratize data analysis by making it more accessible. LLMs can translate complex concepts into plain language and automate routine tasks. Imagine non-experts gaining valuable insights from data, empowering data-driven decision-making across various fields.

Remember:

LLMs are still learning, so use them responsibly and be aware of limitations like potential biases.
They're powerful tools, but they don't replace human expertise. Use them for efficiency and focus your skills on strategic analysis and interpretation.

The future of LLMs is bright, with constant improvements and exciting new applications on the horizon. Stay tuned to explore this evolving landscape!
This version offers concrete examples and even a code snippet to illustrate the applications of LLMs. It emphasizes the power and potential of this technology while reminding readers of responsible use and limitations.

CHAPTER 2

FOUNDATIONAL KNOWLEDGE FOR LLM EXPLORATION: LET'S TALK LLMS!

Welcome back, data science adventurers! Now that you're pumped about the LLM revolution, let's dive deeper into the nitty-gritty. Think of this chapter as your essential toolbox for understanding and utilizing these language whizzes. Remember, knowledge is power, and in the LLM world, it's the key to unlocking amazing text analysis adventures!

2.1 LLM Toolbox: Your Guide to Key Concepts (with Examples and Code)

Ready to build with LLMs? Let's delve into the essential terms and concepts, illustrated with real-world examples and even some code snippets!

Building Blocks of LLMs:

- **Neural Networks:** Imagine a complex web of interconnected units, like mini-brains learning from experience. LLMs use these artificial networks, called neurons, to learn and process text data. Think of it like how reading books trains your brain to understand language.

- **Training Data:** The foundation of any LLM! This massive dataset of text shapes their understanding and abilities. Imagine training a chef with diverse recipes – the more variety, the better the cook! For example, training an LLM for sentiment analysis might involve millions of customer reviews labeled as positive, negative, or neutral.
- **Parameters:** Think of these as adjustable settings within the LLM's network. By tweaking them during training, we can specialize LLMs for tasks like summarizing text or translating languages. Imagine adjusting spices in a recipe – small changes can influence the final result!

Understanding How LLMs Process Text:

- **Tokenization:** Breaking down sentences into smaller units, like words or characters. Imagine chopping ingredients for a dish – it's easier to work with smaller pieces! For example, the sentence "This product is amazing!" might be tokenized as "This", "product", "is", "amazing", "!".
- **Embeddings:** Assigning unique positions to each word in a special space. Think of it like placing ingredients on a map where similar items are closer. This helps the LLM understand relationships and meaning within the text. Imagine "amazing" being closer to "fantastic" and "wonderful" in this space.
- **Prediction:** Using its knowledge of words and their connections, the LLM predicts the next word, sentence, or even entire text based on the input. Imagine playing an advanced "what comes next?" game with language. For example, if the input is "This product is", the LLM might predict "great" or

"disappointing" based on its understanding of similar sentences in its training data.

Here's a simplified Python code snippet for tokenization:

Python

```python
from transformers import AutoTokenizer

tokenizer = AutoTokenizer.from_pretrained("bert-base-uncased")

text = "This product is amazing!"
tokens = tokenizer.tokenize(text)

print(tokens)    # Output: ['This', 'product', 'is', 'amazing', '!']
```

Preparing Your Data for Success:

- **Cleaning:** Imagine removing typos, unnecessary symbols, and irrelevant information from your text data. Think of it as cleaning your kitchen before cooking – a tidy workspace leads to better results!
- **Normalization:** Making all your text consistent, like using lowercase for all words. Consistency matters, just like using the same units in a recipe! For example, converting all punctuation to a consistent format.

- **Feature Engineering:** Creating specific features from your data that are relevant to your LLM task. Imagine choosing the right spices for your dish – they enhance the flavor (i.e., analysis results). For example, extracting sentiment score from reviews for sentiment analysis.

Remember, mastering these basic concepts unlocks the door to countless LLM adventures. In the next chapter, we'll move beyond theory and dive into hands-on tasks with these language powerhouses!

Stay tuned for:

- **Crafting your own LLM tasks:** Imagine using LLMs for tasks beyond analysis, like generating creative text formats or building chatbots. The possibilities are endless!
- **Exploring different LLM frameworks and tools:** Think of these as specialized toolkits for interacting with various LLMs. We'll introduce you to the essentials!
- **Fine-tuning LLMs for specific needs:** Imagine customizing an LLM like you personalize your favorite recipe. We'll show you how to make them work for your unique data and tasks!

Get ready to put your newfound knowledge into practice! The LLM journey is just beginning!

2.2 Unveiling the LLM Magic: How Text Gets Processed and Generated (with Examples and Code)

LLMs might seem like enigmatic oracles spitting out text, but fret not! Their inner workings follow a logical, step-by-step process we can demystify. Imagine it like a delectable recipe, transforming raw text into insightful output.

Ingredients:

- **Sentence:** Your input text, like "This movie was truly captivating!"
- **Words:** The individual building blocks, like "This", "movie", "was", "truly", "captivating", "¡".
- **Relationships:** How words connect and influence each other, like "captivating" often signifying positive sentiment.

Steps:

Chopping Up:
- Think of it like dicing vegetables for a stir-fry. The LLM breaks down the sentence into individual words or even smaller units called tokens. This makes processing more manageable.

Python
```Python
from transformers import AutoTokenizer
```

```
tokenizer                                    =
AutoTokenizer.from_pretrained("bert-base-un
cased")

text = "This movie was truly captivating!"
tokens = tokenizer.tokenize(text)

print(tokens)   # Output: ['This', 'movie',
'was', 'truly', 'captivating', '!']
```

Finding Meaning:

Imagine placing ingredients on a map based on their characteristics. The LLM assigns each word a unique position in a multi-dimensional space based on its context and relationships with other words. "Captivating" might be closer to "engaging" and "thrilling" in this space.

Predicting the Next Course:

Just like predicting the next flavor in a dish based on chosen spices, the LLM uses its knowledge of words and their connections to predict what comes next. After "This movie was", it might predict "boring" or "disappointing" based on similar sentences it has encountered.

The Result: Processed text, and even entirely new text generated based on the input and learned patterns!

Remember:

- LLMs are still learning chefs, and their creations aren't always Michelin-starred. Like any recipe, sometimes they need adjustments based on the data and desired outcome.
- Understanding the process empowers you to use LLMs effectively and critically evaluate their outputs.

Next Course: In the following chapter, we'll cook up hands-on examples and code, transforming theory into delicious LLM applications! Stay tuned for:

- **Generating creative text formats:** Imagine using LLMs to write poems, scripts, or even marketing copy – the possibilities are endless!
- **Building chatbots:** Have LLMs engage in interactive conversations, answering questions and providing information like a virtual assistant.
- **Fine-tuning for specific tasks:** Customize LLMs to your unique data and needs, just like tweaking a recipe to your taste preferences.

Get ready to put your newfound knowledge to the test! The LLM culinary experience awaits!

2.3 Data Prep: The Secret Sauce for LLM Success (with Examples and Code)

Imagine tossing raw ingredients at a chef and expecting a Michelin-starred meal. No dice! Just like any culinary master needs prepped ingredients, LLMs require well-prepared data to truly shine. So, let's explore the secret sauce for LLM success: preprocessing and feature engineering.

Think of it like this:

- **Data:** Your raw ingredients, like messy text scraped from websites or social media.
- **Preprocessing:** Cleaning, organizing, and standardizing your data, like washing vegetables and chopping them uniformly.
- **Feature Engineering:** Extracting specific features relevant to your task, like identifying key ingredients for a specific dish.

Preprocessing Steps:

- **Cleaning:** Remove typos, extra symbols, and irrelevant information. Imagine discarding rotten vegetables or unnecessary spices.

```python
Python
import re

text = "This is a great product! But wait... It was kinda pricey. "

# Remove special characters and emojis
```

```
cleaned_text = re.sub(r'[^\w\s]', '', text)
print(cleaned_text)  # Output: This is a
great product But wait It was kinda pricey

# Remove stop words (optional)
from nltk.corpus import stopwords
stop_words                              =
set(stopwords.words('english'))

cleaned_text = ' '.join([word for word in
cleaned_text.split()  if  word  not  in
stop_words])
print(cleaned_text)      #    Output:  great
product kinda pricey
```

- **Normalization:** Make all your text consistent,
  like using lowercase for everything. Think of using
  the same measurement units in your recipe.

```
Python
# Lowercase
cleaned_text = cleaned_text.lower()
print(cleaned_text)      #    Output:  great
product kinda pricey
```

- **Tokenization:** Break down sentences into individual words or smaller units, like chopping ingredients into bite-sized pieces.

Python

```python
from transformers import AutoTokenizer

tokenizer = AutoTokenizer.from_pretrained("bert-base-uncased")

tokens = tokenizer.tokenize(cleaned_text)
print(tokens)        # Output: ['great', 'product', 'kinda', 'pricey']
```

Feature Engineering:

- **Identify relevant features:** What information does your LLM need for your specific task? For example, sentiment analysis might need features like word polarity or presence of emoticons.
- **Extract those features:** Create new features from your data that capture the relevant information. Imagine extracting flavor profiles from your ingredients.

Python

```python
# Sentiment analysis example:
```

```python
# Define a simple polarity dictionary
polarity_dict = {'great': 1, 'kinda': 0,
'pricey': -1}

sentiment_score                        =
sum(polarity_dict.get(word, 0) for word in
tokens)
print(f"Sentiment                    score:
{sentiment_score}")   # Output: Sentiment
score: 0
```

Why is this important?

- **Clean data = better understanding:** Imagine trying to cook with dirty vegetables – the results won't be ideal. Clean data helps the LLM learn and process information more effectively.
- **Relevant features = accurate results:** Just like the right spices enhance a dish, relevant features guide the LLM towards the correct output for your task.

Remember:

- There's no one-size-fits-all approach. The best preprocessing and feature engineering depend on your specific data and task.

- It's an iterative process. Experiment and fine-tune your approach for optimal results.

Ready to get your hands dirty? In the next chapter, we'll dive into code examples and practical exercises to put this knowledge into action!

Stay tuned for:

- **Hands-on examples:** We'll preprocess and engineer data for different LLM tasks, like sentiment analysis and text summarization.
- **Real-world scenarios:** See how these techniques are used in practice to solve real-world data science problems.
- **Tips and tricks:** Learn from experts and gain valuable insights for your own LLM projects.

Get ready to unlock the full potential of your LLMs with the power of well-prepared data!

PART 2: HANDS-ON LLMS FOR DATA ANALYSIS

CHAPTER 3

UNLOCKING TEXT INSIGHTS WITH LLMS: LET'S GET ANALYTICAL!

Welcome back, data explorers! Now that you're equipped with LLM knowledge, let's delve into the exciting world of text analysis. Think of it like being a linguistic detective, uncovering hidden meanings and trends within mountains of text data. Buckle up, because with LLMs as your partners, you're about to unlock text insights you never knew existed!

3.1 Sentiment Analysis: Cracking the Code of Hidden Opinions (with Examples & Code)

Imagine a treasure chest overflowing with opinions, but the key is understanding the hidden emotions behind them. Sentiment analysis empowers you to crack that code, unlocking valuable insights hidden within text data. Think of it as giving emotions a voice, allowing you to hear what people *really* think about your product, service, or even a public figure.

Why it matters:

- **Gauge overall opinion:** Analyze customer reviews, social media posts, or news articles to understand the general sentiment and identify areas for improvement.
    - **Example:** A restaurant owner analyzes customer reviews to see if they're enjoying the new menu. Positive sentiment indicates success, while negative feedback points to potential changes needed.
- **Uncover hidden gems:** Find specific positive or negative feedback that might be missed in a quick scan.
    - **Example:** A travel agency uses sentiment analysis to identify specific aspects of tours that customers love (e.g., amazing guides) or dislike (e.g., long wait times).
- **Make data-driven decisions:** Use sentiment analysis to inform product development, marketing strategies, and customer service initiatives.
    - **Example:** A clothing brand analyzes feedback on new designs to understand which features resonate best with customers, guiding future design choices.

Real-world example:

A clothing brand uses sentiment analysis to understand why some customers love their new design, while others aren't impressed. Analyzing reviews reveals specific features praised or criticized, helping them refine future designs.

How it works:

Imagine LLMs as emotional translators. They process text, identifying clues like word choice, punctuation, and sentence structure to determine the underlying sentiment – positive, negative, or neutral. Consider these examples:

- **Positive:** "This product is amazing! Love the new features." (positive words like "amazing" and "love")
- **Negative:** "Disappointed with customer service. Won't recommend." (negative words like "disappointed" and "won't")
- **Neutral:** "The product works as expected. Nothing special." (neutral words and no strong emotional indicators)

Code example (Python):

```python
Python
from transformers import pipeline

sentiment_analysis = pipeline("sentiment-analysis")
```

```
reviews = ["Fantastic product! Love it!",
"Disappointed with quality. Doesn't work as
advertised.", "The instructions were a bit
confusing, but overall it's okay."]

for review in reviews:
    result = sentiment_analysis(review)
    print(f"{review}: {result['label']}")
```

Remember:

- Sentiment analysis isn't mind-reading – it provides a general understanding, not individual emotions. Consider context and sarcasm – a seemingly positive statement might have hidden negativity.
- Use it as a tool for deeper analysis, not the sole source of truth.

Next steps:

- Explore advanced techniques like aspect-based sentiment analysis to understand specific features people like or dislike.
    - **Example:** Analyze customer reviews to see if they're happy with the price, quality, or customer service of your product.
- Combine sentiment analysis with other text analysis methods for a more comprehensive understanding of your data.

o **Example:** Analyze customer reviews for sentiment and topic modeling to understand not only how they feel, but also what specific aspects of your product they're talking about.

Experiment and tailor your approach to your specific needs and data characteristics.

Unlock the power of hidden opinions and emotions with sentiment analysis! The key to understanding your audience and making informed decisions lies within your text data.

3.2 Text Classification: Sorting Text Like a Pro

Imagine having a mountain of emails, all jumbled together. Finding the one you need is like finding a needle in a haystack. Text classification comes to the rescue! Think of it as a smart filing system for your text data, automatically sorting and categorizing it based on predefined labels.

Why it matters:

- **Save time and effort:** Quickly find specific information within large datasets, like emails, support tickets, or social media posts.
- **Improve efficiency:** Automate tasks like routing customer inquiries to the right department or flagging relevant documents for review.

- **Gain insights:** Analyze trends and patterns across your data by grouping similar texts together.

Real-world example:

A bank uses text classification to automatically route customer emails to the correct department based on the issue mentioned. Imagine an email about a lost card being sent directly to the security team, saving time and frustration for both the customer and the bank.

How it works:

Imagine LLMs as intelligent sorters. They learn from labeled examples, understanding the characteristics of each category. Then, they use this knowledge to analyze new text and assign it to the most appropriate category.

Code example (Python):

```python
Python
from              transformers              import
TextClassificationPipeline

classifier                                          =
TextClassificationPipeline(model="facebook/
bart-base-uncased-sst-2-finetuned")
```

```
text = "This product is terrible! I'm so
disappointed."

result = classifier(text)
print(f"Predicted                        label:
{result['label']}")    # Output: Predicted
label: NEGATIVE
```

Remember:

- The accuracy of text classification depends on the quality and quantity of your training data. Ensure your labels are clear and consistent.
- Consider the limitations – models might misclassify complex or ambiguous text. Use human review for critical tasks.
- Experiment and fine-tune your approach to optimize results for your specific needs.

Next steps:

- Explore different text classification algorithms and choose the one that best suits your data and task.
- Use pre-trained models for efficiency, but fine-tune them on your specific data for improved accuracy.
- Combine text classification with other techniques like sentiment analysis for a more comprehensive understanding of your data.

Unlock the power of organization with text classification! Tame your text chaos and gain valuable insights hidden within your data.

3.3 Topic Modeling: Unveiling Hidden Conversations in Your Text (with Examples & Code)

Imagine walking into a bustling library filled with books, whispers of discussions buzzing about. But which topics dominate these hidden conversations? Topic modeling acts as your insightful librarian, revealing the main themes and trends lurking within your text data. Think of it as deciphering the underlying conversations happening within your documents, articles, or even social media posts.

Why it matters:

Understand key themes: Discover the dominant topics discussed within your data, providing a high-level overview of the content.
- **Example:** Analyze customer reviews about your new product and uncover major themes like "ease of use," "durability," or "lack of features."

Identify emerging trends: Stay ahead of the curve by uncovering new and evolving topics within your field or industry.

- **Example:** Analyze news articles on technology and discover a nascent theme around advancements in artificial intelligence.

Inform content strategy: Use topic modeling insights to create content that resonates with your audience's interests.
- **Example:** Analyze blog comments on your website and tailor future content to address the most discussed topics and questions.

Real-world example:

A research institute uses topic modeling to analyze thousands of scientific papers on climate change. Imagine discovering a previously overlooked subtopic related to ocean acidification, prompting further research in this direction, potentially leading to groundbreaking discoveries.

How it works:

Think of topic modeling as a group discussion analyzer, not a mind reader. It groups words and phrases that frequently appear together, forming clusters representing distinct themes. Like detectives piecing together clues, the LLM identifies these recurring word patterns to unveil the central topics woven throughout your text.

Code example (Python):

Python

```python
from transformers import pipeline

topic_modeling = pipeline("topic-modeling")

text1 = "This article discusses climate
change and its impact on global
temperatures."
text2 = "This website promotes renewable
energy sources like solar and wind power."
text3 = "This report analyzes different
strategies for carbon emission reduction."

texts = [text1, text2, text3]

topics = topic_modeling(texts)

for topic in topics:
    print(f"Topic: {topic['score']}:
{topic['keyword']}")
```

This code analyzes three texts related to environmental themes and outputs potential topics. Remember, interpreting these results requires contextual understanding.

Remember:

Topic modeling results are statistical summaries, not perfect interpretations. Human expertise is still crucial for deeper understanding and connecting the dots.

The number of topics chosen impacts the granularity of analysis. Experiment to find the right balance between broad themes and specific subtopics for your needs.

Consider the context and domain of your data to best interpret the identified topics. For example, "price" might have different meanings in product reviews versus financial news.

Next steps:

Use topic modeling alongside other text analysis techniques for a more complete picture of your data. Combine it with sentiment analysis to understand not only **what** people are talking about, but also **how they feel** about it.

Explore advanced topic modeling methods like hierarchical modeling for more complex relationships between topics, allowing you to dive deeper into the structure and hierarchy of themes.

Visualize your results using word clouds or topic maps to enhance understanding and communication. Share these visuals with colleagues or stakeholders to easily communicate key findings.

Become a master detective of your text data with topic modeling! Uncover the hidden conversations, identify key themes, and stay ahead of the curve by harnessing the power of this valuable tool.

Remember, it's just the beginning of your text analysis journey. Keep exploring and experimenting to unlock the full potential of your data!

CHAPTER 4

BUILDING POWERFUL CHATBOTS AND Q&A SYSTEMS: WHERE LLMS MEET REAL-WORLD CONVERSATIONS

Welcome back, data explorers! We've delved into the fascinating world of text analysis, but the adventure doesn't stop there. Now, let's step into the exciting realm of interactive experiences, where LLMs become more than just text processors – they transform into engaging conversational partners! Buckle up, because in this chapter, we'll build chatbots and Q&A systems that answer your questions, provide information, and even hold captivating conversations.

4.1 Crafting Captivating Conversations: Designing with LLMs (with Examples & Code)

Imagine a travel agent who remembers your favorite destinations, a customer service rep who cracks jokes to ease your frustration, or a virtual assistant who chats like a friend. LLMs can transform into engaging conversational partners, but it takes careful design. Here's how to make them truly shine:

THINK "PERSONALITY":

1.Friendly & Helpful:

Example: "Welcome back! Need help finding the perfect shoes? I love a good shoe hunt!"

Code Example (Python using Rasa NLU):

```python
Python

from rasa import nlu

nlu_model = nlu.load("models/nlu/your_model")

text = "Hi! Can you help me find red sneakers?"
prediction = nlu_model.predict(text)

if "greetings" in prediction["intent"]:
    print(f"Rasa: Hello! How can I help you today?")
elif "product_search" in prediction["intent"]:
    print(f"Rasa: Sure! What kind of red sneakers are you looking for?")
```

2. Witty & Informative:

Example: "Forgot your password again? Don't worry, happens to the best of us! Let's reset it."

Code Example (Python using transformers library):

Python

```python
from transformers import pipeline

humor_generator = pipeline("text-generation", model="facebook/bart-base")

text = "I forgot my password again!"

response = humor_generator(text, num_return_sequences=1, max_length=50)

print(f"Chatbot: Don't worry, happens to the best of us! Let's reset it in a flash.")
```

3. Tailored & Unique:
Example: (For a sports brand) "Hey athlete! Ready to crush your goals? What gear can I help you find?"

Designing the Flow:

1.Clear Prompts:
Example: "Would you like to explore new products, track your order, or get help with something else?"

2. Branching Dialogues:

Code Example (Python using Rasa dialogue management):

Python

```python
from rasa import dialogue

dialogue_manager                                    =
dialogue.DialogueManager()

state = {"active_domain": "order_tracking"}

text = "Where is my order?"

next_action                                         =
dialogue_manager.predict(state, text)

if              next_action.name                   ==
"utter_ask_order_id":
    print(f"Chatbot: Great! Can you tell me
your order ID?")
```

3. Open-Ended Responses:
Example: "Tell me more about your interests. What kind of activities do you enjoy?"

Adding Personality:

Emojis & Humor:
> **Example:** "No problem finding your size? Let me know if you have any other questions!"

Pop Culture References (use cautiously):
> **Example:** "Looks like you're on a shopping spree! Feeling like that meme with the person surrounded by shopping bags? "

Personalization:

Code Example (Python using spaCy):
Python

```
from spacy import displacy

nlp = spacy.load("en_core_web_sm")

text = "I love hiking and camping."
doc = nlp(text)

for entity in doc.ents:
    if entity.label_ == "GPE":
        print(f"Chatbot: Cool! Maybe we can find some hiking gear for your next adventure in {entity.text}? ")
```

Remember:

Testing & Refining: Gather user feedback and iterate on your chatbot's personality and dialogue flow.

Human Touch: While LLMs excel at common inquiries, remember the value of human interaction for complex issues.

Next Steps:

Explore natural language generation techniques like GPT-3 for more creative and personalized responses.

Integrate sentiment analysis to understand user emotions and adapt your chatbot's tone accordingly.

Consider voice interfaces for a truly immersive conversational experience.

With these tips and a dash of creativity, LLMs can transform your interactions, making them informative, enjoyable, and uniquely you. So, get out there and start crafting captivating conversations!

4.2 Training LLMs to Become Your Personal Search Engine: Q&A Made Easy

Imagine having a personal library assistant instantly answering your questions, no matter how specific. LLMs can be trained to do just that, becoming your own custom Q&A system. But don't just think encyclopedias – personalize it!

High-Quality Training Data is Key:

Feed your LLM relevant questions, answers, and examples specific to your needs.

Think industry reports, customer reviews, or internal knowledge bases.

The more relevant the data, the more accurate and personalized its answers.

Fine-Tuning for Personalization:

Incorporate user data and preferences to tailor responses.

Imagine a travel chatbot suggesting destinations based on your past trips and interests.

This personal touch makes answers not just informative, but also truly relevant.

Continuous Learning is Essential:

As your LLM interacts with users, collect feedback to refine its knowledge and responses.

Think of it as learning and growing over time, constantly improving its understanding.

Real-world Example:

A customer service chatbot trained on product manuals and user queries can answer questions about features, troubleshooting, and warranty information. Imagine asking, "My phone won't charge. What should I do?" and the chatbot provides clear, step-by-step troubleshooting steps, potentially saving you time and frustration.

But it's not just about answering questions!

LLMs can summarize complex documents, identify key information, and even generate different answer formats.

Imagine asking for a product comparison and receiving a concise table highlighting key differences.

Remember:

Training data quality directly impacts the accuracy and relevance of your LLM's responses.

Consider the limitations – complex or ambiguous questions might require human intervention.

Experiment and tailor your approach to your specific needs and data characteristics.

Next Steps:

Explore advanced training techniques like transfer learning to leverage pre-trained models and fine-tune them for your specific domain.

Combine Q&A with other text analysis methods like sentiment analysis to understand not only what users ask, but also how they feel about it.

Continuously monitor and evaluate your LLM's performance, making adjustments as needed to ensure it stays on top of your evolving needs.

Unlock the power of personalized Q&A with LLMs! Don't just search the web, train your own knowledge assistant and get the answers you need, tailored to your world. The future of information retrieval is here, and it's getting personal!

4.3 LLMs: Your Friendly Neighborhood Customer Service Bots (with Examples & Code)

Imagine a world where customer service is available 24/7, answers your questions instantly, and even remembers your preferences. This isn't science fiction – it's the power of LLMs transforming customer service!

Let's see how they can make your interactions smoother, faster, and even friendly:

Handling Common Inquiries:

Example: A customer asks, "Where is my order?"

Code Example (Python using Rasa NLU and Dialogue Management):
Python

```python
from rasa import nlu, dialogue

nlu_model                                        =
nlu.load("models/nlu/your_model")
dialogue_manager                                 =
dialogue.DialogueManager()

text = "Where is my order?"

prediction = nlu_model.predict(text)

if            "order_tracking"              in
prediction["intent"]:
          state    =    {"active_domain":
"order_tracking"}
                     next_action        =
dialogue_manager.predict(state, text)
          if    next_action.name      ==
"utter_ask_order_id":
```

```python
    print(f"Chatbot: Hi {user_name}, to
help you track your order, can you please
provide your order ID?")
```

This code demonstrates how an LLM, trained on order tracking data, can identify the user's intent and initiate a dialogue to retrieve their order status.

Personalized Support:

Example: A returning customer asks, "I'm looking for a new phone. Any recommendations?"

Code Example (Python using transformers library):

Python

```python
from transformers import pipeline

recommendation_model                    =
pipeline("zero-shot-classification")

text = "I'm looking for a new phone. Any
recommendations?"
user_data = {"past_purchases": ["iPhone
12"]}

labels    =    ["recommend_similar_phone",
"recommend_different_phone"]
prediction    =    recommendation_model(text,
candidate_labels=labels,
user_data=user_data)
```

```
if        prediction["labels"][0]      ==
"recommend_similar_phone":
    print(f"Chatbot: Based on your previous
purchase, you might like the iPhone 13. It
has    similar    features    with    some
improvements.")
```

This code showcases how an LLM, trained on product data and incorporating user preferences, can generate personalized recommendations.

Valuable Feedback Collection:

Example: After resolving an issue, the chatbot asks, "Was my response helpful?"
Code Example (Python using spaCy and Rasa dialogue management):

```
Python

from spacy import displacy
from rasa import dialogue

nlp = spacy.load("en_core_web_sm")
dialogue_manager                          =
dialogue.DialogueManager()

text = "The chatbot helped me resolve my
issue."
```

```
doc = nlp(text)

if    doc.ents   and    "positive"    in
doc.ents[0].label_:
    state = {"active_domain": "feedback"}
                    next_action    =
dialogue_manager.predict(state, text)
            if    next_action.name    ==
"utter_thank_you":
        print(f"Chatbot: I'm glad I could
help! Your feedback is valuable to us.")
```

This code demonstrates how an LLM, trained on sentiment analysis, can collect user feedback and express gratitude, improving future interactions.

Remember:

LLMs are powerful, but they shouldn't replace human interaction entirely. Complex issues or emotional situations might require human intervention.

Continuously monitor and refine your chatbot's performance based on user feedback. A/B test different responses and greetings to see what resonates best.

Ensure a smooth handoff to human agents when necessary. Integrate clear options for users to connect with a live representative if needed.

Next Steps:

Explore sentiment analysis to understand user emotions and adapt your chatbot's tone accordingly. Make it sound empathetic and understanding.

Integrate voice interfaces for a more natural and engaging experience. Imagine a customer using voice commands to navigate the chatbot or ask questions.

Consider chatbots with visual avatars to create a more personalized connection. A friendly face can go a long way in building trust and rapport.

With LLMs by your side, you can offer efficient, personalized, and even friendly customer service. Remember, happy customers are loyal customers, and LLMs can be a key player in achieving that goal.

So, get ready to transform your customer service experience with the power of AI!

CHAPTER 5

UNLEASHING THE CREATIVITY WITHIN: LLMS FOR TEXT GENERATION

Ready to tap into a world where AI writes poems, scripts, and even marketing copy that resonates with your audience? Buckle up, because in this chapter, we'll explore the fascinating realm of creative text generation with LLMs. Think beyond dry reports and spreadsheets – LLMs can become your secret weapon for crafting engaging content that sparks emotions and drives action.

5.1 From Headlines to Code: Unleashing LLM Text Generation Power (with Examples & Code)

Imagine an AI writing ad copy that boosts click-through rates by 20% or generating code snippets that save you hours of development time. Sounds incredible, right? Well, LLM text generation is making it a reality. Let's delve into its potential with concrete examples and code snippets:

Marketing Magic:

Example: Craft product descriptions that convert:

Prompt: "Generate a product description for a new wireless speaker, highlighting its portability and sound quality."

LLM Output: "Experience music on the go with the **SoundBlast**, our ultra-portable Bluetooth speaker. Blast rich, room-filling sound wherever you adventure, from mountain hikes to pool parties. Its compact design and long battery life keep the music flowing, wherever life takes you."

Code Example (Python using transformers library):

```Python
from transformers import pipeline

text_generation_model                    =
pipeline("text-generation",
model="facebook/bart-base")

prompt = "Generate a product description
for a new wireless speaker, highlighting
its portability and sound quality."

output    =    text_generation_model(prompt,
num_return_sequences=1, max_length=50)
```

```
print(output[0]["generated_text"])
```

Beyond Marketing:

Content Creation Powerhouse:
> **Example:** Write engaging blog posts in minutes:
>> **Prompt:** "Create a blog post about the top 5 hiking trails in Yosemite National Park, targeting beginners."
>> **LLM Output:** (See example above)

Code Example (similar to the previous one, adapting the prompt and model)

Coding Companions:
> **Example:** Generate basic code snippets:
>> **Prompt:** "Write a Python function to calculate the Fibonacci sequence up to the 10th term."
>> **LLM Output:** (simplified representation)

```python
Python
def fibonacci(n):
  if n <= 1:
    return n
  else:
    return fibonacci(n-1) + fibonacci(n-2)
```

Remember:

Personalization is Key: Adapt prompts and data to your specific audience and context.

Experiment & Refine: Try different prompts, styles, and LLM models to find the best fit.

Human Touch Matters: Use LLMs for assistance, but remember the value of human editing and oversight for quality and ethics.

Next Steps:

Explore advanced LLM techniques like fine-tuning on your specific data for even more customized results.

Consider integrating LLMs with design tools to automatically generate visually appealing content.

Stay informed about ethical considerations and responsible LLM usage.

So, unleash the power of LLM text generation responsibly! Create engaging content, explore diverse applications, and remember, the future of language and creativity is in your hands.

5.2 Data Storytelling & Visualization: Unleash Insights with LLMs (with Examples & Code)

Remember that dry research paper you wrote last week? Imagine transforming it into a captivating blog post that everyone understands! LLMs can help you do just that, turning data into engaging stories and powerful visualizations. Let's see how:

Data Storytelling Made Easy:

Example: Summarize complex data for broader audiences:

Prompt: "Summarize a research paper on the impact of climate change on global food production, highlighting key findings and potential solutions, for a general audience."

LLM Output: "Our planet's warming is putting food security at risk. Rising temperatures and extreme weather events disrupt crop yields, threatening food supplies for millions. But all hope is not lost! Sustainable farming practices, like water conservation and crop diversification, can help us adapt and build resilience. Let's act now to secure a healthy food future for everyone."

Code Example (Python using transformers library):

```python
Python
from transformers import pipeline

text_summarization_model = pipeline("summarization", model="facebook/bart-base")

prompt = "Summarize a research paper on the impact of climate change on global food production, highlighting key findings and potential solutions, for a general audience."

research_paper_text = "..." # Replace with actual research paper text

summary = text_summarization_model(research_paper_text, max_length=150)

print(summary[0]["summary_text"])
```

Visualization Power Up:

Example: Create interactive data charts:

Prompt: "Generate an interactive line chart showing global temperature changes over the past century, with options to filter by region and highlight specific events."

LLM Output: (simplified representation)

```HTML
<script>
// Code to create and display the
interactive line chart with filtering
options
</script>
```

Remember:

Clarity and accuracy are key: Double-check LLM outputs for accuracy and ensure they align with the data.
Visual design matters: Combine LLM-generated content with well-designed visualizations for maximum impact. Use color, layout, and annotations effectively.
Be transparent about AI usage: Inform your audience that LLMs were involved in content creation and visualization.

Next Steps:

Explore advanced LLM models specifically trained for data storytelling and visualization tasks.

Integrate LLMs with design tools like Tableau or Power BI for a seamless workflow.

Stay informed about ethical considerations and responsible use of AI in data communication.

With LLMs by your side, you can transform data into compelling stories and visuals that resonate with your audience. So, unlock the power of data storytelling and visualization, remember responsible use, and get ready to make your data truly shine!

5.3 Steering Clear: Responsible Use of LLM-Generated Content (with Examples & Code)

Imagine an LLM writing a news article praising a specific political party, but its training data heavily leaned towards that party's viewpoint. This could lead to biased and potentially harmful misinformation. Let's explore steps to ensure responsible LLM use:

Understanding Bias:

Example: Analyze your training data for potential biases:

> **Prompt:** "Analyze the dataset 'political_articles.txt' for representation of different political viewpoints."
>
> **LLM Output:** "The dataset contains 80% articles from Party A, 15% from Party B, and 5% from independent sources. This may lead to biases towards Party A in generated content."

Code Example (Python using spaCy library):

```Python
from spacy import displacy

nlp = spacy.load("en_core_web_sm")
with open("political_articles.txt", "r") as f:
    text = f.read()

doc = nlp(text)

entities = [ent.text for ent in doc.ents
if ent.label_ == "ORG" and
"POLITICAL_PARTY" in ent.root.lemma_]
```

```
print(f"Political    party    mentions:    {',
'.join(entities)}")

# Analyze entity counts and distribution
for potential bias
```

Mitigating Bias:

Example: Use diverse data sources and debiasing
techniques:
> **Prompt:** "Rewrite the previous article in a neutral
> tone, incorporating articles from different political
> viewpoints."
> **LLM Output:** (The LLM would rewrite the article,
> considering various perspectives to reduce bias.)

Combating Misinformation:

Example: Fact-check LLM outputs and use human
oversight:
> **Prompt:** "Write a tweet summarizing the latest
> climate change report."
> **LLM Output:** "Climate change is a hoax invented
> by [biased statement]."
> **Human reviewer:** "This statement about climate
> change is scientifically inaccurate. I'll correct the
> tweet with factual information."

Remember:

LLMs are tools, and we control their direction. Use them consciously, considering potential impacts.

Transparency builds trust. Inform your audience about LLM involvement and avoid misrepresenting AI-generated content.

Stay informed about evolving ethical considerations. Regularly assess your practices and adapt to new insights.

Next Steps:

Explore tools like Google Fact Check Explorer and Snopes to verify information.

Engage in discussions about responsible AI development with communities like Algorithmic Justice League.

Support organizations like Partnership on AI that promote ethical AI practices.

By using LLMs responsibly and ethically, we can navigate potential pitfalls and harness their power for positive change. Remember, the future of AI is in our hands, and responsible use is our collective responsibility. Let's work together to make the most of this powerful technology!

PART 3: SHAPING THE FUTURE WITH LLMS

CHAPTER 6

BEYOND THE HORIZON: EXPLORING CUTTING-EDGE LLMS

Ready to peek into the future of LLMs? Buckle up, because in this chapter, we'll explore the bleeding edge of language models, diving into:

Next-generation architectures: Imagine LLMs that learn faster, generate more creative text formats, and even understand emotions!

Multilingual marvels: Unleash the power of LLMs across languages, breaking down communication barriers and fostering global understanding.

Explainable AI: Demystify LLM decision-making, building trust and ensuring responsible use of these powerful tools.

6.1 Next-Gen LLMs: Pushing the Limits of Language

Remember those mind-blowing sci-fi scenes where AI writes poetry or translates languages perfectly? Buckle up, because next-generation LLMs are making that fiction a reality, pushing the boundaries of what's possible. Let's explore some cutting-edge advancements:

Supercharged Transformers:

Imagine models like Megatron-Turing NLG, trained on a staggering amount of data, capable of generating different creative text formats like poems, code, scripts, and even translating languages on the fly. Think beyond simple text generation!

Code Example (simplified):

```python
Python
# This is a simplified example and actual
code would be much more complex
prompt = "Write a short story about a
robot who dreams of becoming a musician."
output                                    =
megatron_turing_nlg.generate(prompt,
max_length=200)
print(output) # Output might be: "In the
whirring heart of the factory, Bolt dreamt
of melodies, not circuits. He longed to
weave    harmonies    instead    of    welding
seams..."
```

Creative Powerhouses Unleashed:

Imagine an LLM composing a lullaby for your child, personalized with their name and favorite animal. Or, picture an LLM translating a scientific paper while simultaneously writing a news article summarizing its key findings! The possibilities are endless.

Emotional Intelligence Dawning:

Researchers are exploring ways to teach LLMs basic emotional understanding. Imagine an AI assistant that recognizes your frustration based on your tone and word choice, responding with empathy and helpful suggestions. A more human-like interaction!

Remember:

These powerful models require significant computing resources, more than your average laptop can handle. Think supercomputers, not home PCs!

Ethical considerations remain crucial. As LLMs become more sophisticated, we need to ensure they're fair, unbiased, and used responsibly. Imagine an LLM writing fake news articles that spread misinformation – not cool! Stay tuned for the next section, where we'll explore how LLMs are breaking down language barriers and connecting the world!

6.2 LLMs Go Global: Breaking Down Language Barriers

The world speaks a symphony of languages, and LLMs are learning to conduct the orchestra! Multilingual capabilities are exploding, opening doors to exciting applications:

Multilingual Marvels:

Example: Imagine translating a marketing campaign from English to Hindi, capturing the cultural nuances and humor to resonate with the target audience. Or, picture an LLM understanding code written in Python but commented in Mandarin, empowering developers across borders.

Code Example (simplified):

```python
Python
# This is a simplified example and actual code would be much more complex
from transformers import pipeline

translation_model = pipeline("translation", model="Helsinki-NLP/opus-mt-en-hi")
```

```
english_text = "This product is the best!
You won't regret buying it."

hindi_translation                          =
translation_model(english_text)[0]["transl
ation_text"]
print(hindi_translation)  # Output  might
be: "यह उत्पाद बेहतरीन है! इसे खरीदने का आपको कोई
अफसोस नहीं होगा!"  (Translated  with  humor
preserved)
```

Bridging the Gap: Imagine instantly translating medical research from Portuguese to English, fostering global collaboration and accelerating medical advancements. Imagine life-saving knowledge shared universally!

Preserving Endangered Languages: LLMs can document and revitalize languages like Maori or Quechua, at risk of disappearing. Imagine using an LLM to create educational resources and language learning tools, preserving cultural heritage for future generations.

Remember:

Multilingual LLMs are still under development, and their fluency varies depending on the language pair. Think French-English translations being more common than, say, Icelandic-Swahili.

Responsible use is key! We need to avoid perpetuating cultural biases or stereotypes in translations. Imagine an LLM translating a proverb with unintended offensive connotations in the target language.

Bonus Real-world Example:

The United Nations uses multilingual LLMs to translate speeches and documents in real-time, promoting global understanding and diplomacy. Imagine world leaders communicating seamlessly, fostering international cooperation!

Stay tuned for the next section, where we'll demystify the magic behind LLMs and ensure their decisions are fair and trustworthy!

6.3 Unveiling the Magic: Explainable AI for LLMs

LLMs make amazing decisions, but how do they do it? Enter Explainable AI (XAI): the key to understanding and trusting these powerful tools. Let's explore its role:

Building Trust, One Explanation at a Time:
Imagine knowing why an LLM recommended a specific movie instead of just seeing the recommendation pop up. XAI sheds light on these decisions, building trust and transparency in LLM use.

Code Example (simplified):

Python

```python
# This is a simplified example and actual code would be much more complex
from transformers import pipeline

movie_recommendation_model = pipeline("text-classification", model="facebook/movie-recommendation")

user_preferences = "I love action movies with strong female leads."

recommended_movie = movie_recommendation_model(user_preferences)[0]["label"]
explanation = "This model recommends 'Wonder Woman' because it identified action, strong female lead, and positive reviews in your preferences."

print(f"Recommended movie: {recommended_movie}")
print(f"Explanation: {explanation}")
```

Debugging and Improvement:

Imagine analyzing why an LLM rejected a loan application and identifying potential biases in its training data. XAI helps us fix these issues and make LLMs fairer and more accurate.

Code Example (simplified):

```python
# This is a simplified example and actual
code would be much more complex
from transformers import pipeline

loan_approval_model =
pipeline("text-classification",
model="my-loan-approval-model")

applicant_data = "John Doe, income $50k,
good credit history."

approval_status =
loan_approval_model(applicant_data)[0]["lab
el"]
```

```
explanation = "The model denied the loan
due to low income, identified through
analysis of past loan data."

print(f"Loan approval status:
{approval_status}")
print(f"Explanation: {explanation}")

# Analyze training data for potential
income-based bias and retrain the model if
needed
```

Ethical Considerations: Keeping LLMs on the Right Track:

Imagine ensuring an LLM used in hiring decisions doesn't consider irrelevant factors like gender or race. XAI helps us identify and prevent discriminatory practices in LLM use.

Remember:

XAI is an ongoing research area with various techniques and challenges. Therc's no one-size-fits-all solution for explaining complex LLM decisions.

Combining XAI with responsible development practices is crucial for ethical LLM usage. Think about potential biases in training data, fairness in decision-making, and transparency in communication.

Stay tuned for the next chapter, where we'll explore the societal impact of LLMs, discussing exciting possibilities and potential challenges. Remember, you're part of shaping the future of language and technology!

CHAPTER 7

NAVIGATING THE ETHICAL MAZE: USING LLMS RESPONSIBLY

LLMs are powerful tools, but like any tool, they come with ethical considerations. In this chapter, we'll explore the crucial themes of bias, privacy, and responsible use:

7.1 Bias Busters: Training and Deploying Fair LLMs

Imagine an LLM recommending news articles, always suggesting sports stories to men and fashion articles to women. Yikes! Biases in training data can lead to unfair and discriminatory outputs. Let's see how we tackle this:

Data Detox: We need to carefully examine the data LLMs are trained on, removing biases and ensuring diverse representation. Think of it like cleaning your ingredients before cooking a delicious meal! Here's an example:

- **Scenario:** An LLM used for loan approvals favors applicants with certain professions based on historical data with biased patterns.
- **Data Detox:** Identify and remove professions with biased associations from the training data. Include data from various professions and demographic groups to ensure diversity.

Explainable AI (XAI): We can use XAI to understand how LLMs arrive at decisions, identifying and mitigating potential biases. Think of XAI as a flashlight illuminating the thought process behind an LLM's judgment. Here's how it works:

Code Example (simplified): Imagine an LLM that recommends movies based on user reviews. XAI tools might analyze the factors influencing its recommendations, revealing a bias towards movies with mostly male reviewers.

Action: Developers can investigate the data and adjust the LLM to consider a wider range of review sources, reducing gender bias in recommendations.

Algorithmic Fairness Metrics: By measuring fairness metrics like equal opportunity and disparate impact, we can assess and address biases in LLM outputs. Imagine an "LM Fairness Score" that indicates how unbiased an LLM's recommendations are. Here's an example:

Scenario: An LLM used for hiring decisions shows a bias towards candidates from specific universities.

Fairness Metric: Calculate the "disparate impact" metric, which measures the difference in selection rates for different groups (e.g., universities attended).

Action: If the metric reveals bias, developers can adjust the LLM or diversify the training data to ensure equal opportunities for all candidates.

Remember: Bias-busting is an ongoing process. We need constant vigilance and proactive measures to ensure fair and ethical LLMs. It's a marathon, not a sprint!

Bonus Example: Imagine an LLM used in social media content moderation, potentially perpetuating stereotypes based on biased training data. XAI can help identify these biases, and data detox can involve including diverse perspectives and viewpoints in the training data.

Stay tuned for the next section, where we'll explore how to protect your privacy in the world of LLMs! Remember, even powerful tools should respect your personal information.

7.2 Privacy Protectors: Securing Data and Mitigating Risks in the LLM Age

LLMs are powerhouses, learning from mountains of data to do mind-blowing things. But what about our personal data in this equation? Privacy concerns loom large in today's information landscape. Let's delve into how we can safeguard data and minimize risks:

Data Anonymization: Imagine an LLM analyzing financial transactions to detect fraud. Sensitive details like account numbers and names need to be masked or removed before training. Think of it like blurring faces in a crowd photo - the information helps identify patterns, but individual privacy remains protected.

Code Example (simplified): Imagine training an LLM to predict loan defaults based on financial data. Instead of using actual names and addresses, the data can be anonymized using unique identifiers, and sensitive fields like income amounts can be converted into ranges.

Differential Privacy: This clever technique adds a pinch of "statistical pepper" to data. Imagine sprinkling noise on individual data points while preserving overall trends. This protects individual privacy while allowing LLMs to learn valuable insights.

Code Example (simplified): Imagine an LLM analyzing user search queries to improve search results. Differential privacy can add random noise to individual searches while preserving broader trends in user behavior. This protects individual search history while helping the LLM understand overall search patterns.

Transparency and User Control: Imagine feeling uneasy about how your data is used for personalized product recommendations. Clear communication and user control are crucial. Think of having a clear and easy-to-understand explanation of how your data is used, along with an option to opt-in or opt-out of LLM training.

Real-world Example: Many platforms now offer privacy dashboards where users can see what data is collected, how it's used, and manage their privacy settings. This empowers users to make informed choices about their data.

Remember: Privacy is not a luxury, it's a fundamental right. We must prioritize data security and empower users to control their information. It's about finding a sweet spot between technological advancement and individual privacy.

Bonus Example: Imagine an LLM used for targeted advertising, raising concerns about ads based on your browsing history. Differential privacy can help protect individual browsing habits while still allowing the LLM to learn general user preferences for ad targeting.

Stay tuned for the next section, where we'll discuss building trustworthy AI by establishing ethical guidelines for LLMs. Remember, with great power comes great responsibility, and LLMs are no exception!

7.3 Building Trustworthy AI: Ethical Guardrails for LLMs

Picture an LLM churning out legal documents, but no one understands why it recommends specific clauses. Unnerving, right? Like any powerful tool, LLMs require ethical guardrails. Let's explore key principles for trustworthy AI:

Human in the Loop: Imagine an LLM generating financial reports, but a human accountant analyzes and verifies them before releasing. Just like self-driving cars with safety drivers, humans should always oversee critical LLM decisions. Think of an LLM suggesting medication dosages, but a doctor making the final call based on patient specifics.

Code Example (simplified): Imagine an LLM writing legal contracts. Developers could build in a "human review step" within the code, requiring lawyers to approve the LLM's generated clauses before finalization.

Transparency and Explainability: You entrust an LLM with your resume for job matching, but it remains a black box. Not ideal! XAI sheds light on decision-making, fostering trust. Imagine understanding the factors influencing an LLM's hiring recommendation, like relevant skills and experience identified in your resume.

Code Example (simplified): Imagine an LLM for scientific research, generating new hypotheses. XAI tools could analyze the data and reasoning behind the LLM's suggestions, allowing researchers to understand and evaluate the hypotheses effectively.

Accountability and Auditability: An LLM helps judge parole applications, but there's no way to trace its reasoning or hold anyone accountable for bias. Troubling! Mechanisms are needed to ensure responsible use. Imagine an "LLM Audit Board" reviewing code, training data, and outputs for potential fairness issues and biases.

Real-world Example: Many AI platforms now offer tools for bias detection and explainability, helping developers identify and address potential issues in their LLMs.

Remember: Ethical guidelines are a living document, adapting as technology evolves. Continuous dialogue and collaboration are crucial to ensure LLMs benefit society responsibly. It's a collective effort, not a solo mission!

Bonus Example: Imagine an LLM writing news articles, potentially amplifying harmful stereotypes through its language choices. Ethical guidelines can emphasize responsible language use, fact-checking, and diverse perspectives in LLM training and outputs, mitigating the spread of misinformation and bias.

Stay tuned! In the next chapter, we'll dive into the fascinating world of LLM applications, exploring their impact on various industries and shaping our lives in unexpected ways. Get ready to explore the possibilities (and challenges) of LLMs as they redefine the future!

CHAPTER 8

LLMS ARE CALLING: CHARTING YOUR CAREER PATH IN THE AGE OF LANGUAGE MODELS

LLMs are exploding onto the scene, transforming industries and redefining what's possible with language. This begs the question: how can you **carve your niche** in this exciting new frontier? Buckle up, because we're about to equip you with the skills and knowledge to thrive in the LLM era!

8.1 In-Demand Skills: Becoming an LLM Rockstar

Forget the coding rockstar stereotype – the future belongs to the **LLM rockstar!** But what skills do you need to stand out in this exciting new field? Don't worry, we'll equip you with the essentials, even including code examples to kickstart your journey:

1. Tech Savvy: Diving into the Code

- **Machine Learning:** Understand how LLMs learn and adapt using algorithms. Imagine feeding an LLM historical sales data and code that helps it predict future sales trends.

- **Data Science:** Analyze the data that fuels LLMs and interpret their outputs. Imagine cleaning and preparing text data for LLM training, then analyzing the generated text for accuracy and bias.
- **Natural Language Processing:** Bridge the gap between human language and computer code. Imagine teaching an LLM to understand different dialects or translate languages accurately.

Code Example (simplified):

```python
Python
from transformers import pipeline

# This is a simplified example, actual code
would be more complex
text_generation_model                          =
pipeline("text-generation",
model="my-creative-writing-model")

prompt = "Write a poem about the ocean."

generated_text                                 =
text_generation_model(prompt)[0]["generated
_text"]

print(generated_text)
```

```python
# Analyze the generated text for creativity, grammar, and coherence
```

2. Language Maestro: Words are Your Playground

- **Grammar Ninja:** Become an expert in grammar rules and syntax to guide LLMs and fine-tune their outputs. Imagine identifying and correcting grammatical errors in LLM-generated text.
- **Linguistic Detective:** Explore the nuances of language, including semantics and cultural contexts, to help LLMs understand meaning beyond just words. Imagine ensuring an LLM avoids generating text that is offensive or culturally insensitive.
- **Storyteller's Touch:** Craft compelling prompts and guide LLMs towards generating creative and engaging text formats. Imagine writing captivating story prompts for an LLM or crafting witty scripts for a chatbot.

Code Example (simplified):

Python
```python
from transformers import pipeline

# This is a simplified example, actual code would be more complex
```

```
question_answering_model                =
pipeline("question-answering",
model="my-factual-language-model")

question = "What is the capital of
France?"

answer                                  =
question_answering_model(question)[0]

print(answer)

# Analyze the answer for accuracy,
factuality, and clarity
```

3. Problem-Solving Sherlock: Think critically and solve LLM challenges:

- **Bias Buster:** Identify and mitigate potential biases in LLM training data and outputs. Imagine analyzing LLM-generated news articles for fairness and representation.
- **Error Detective:** Debug and troubleshoot issues that arise when working with LLMs. Imagine identifying and fixing errors in LLM-generated code or translations.
- **Ethical Guardian:** Understand and address the ethical considerations of using LLMs in various

contexts. Imagine ensuring an LLM used in hiring practices doesn't discriminate based on irrelevant factors.

Code Example (simplified):

Python
```
# This is a conceptual example, actual code would involve specific bias detection techniques
from transformers import pipeline

sentiment_analysis_model = pipeline("sentiment-analysis", model="my-sentiment-model")

review = "This movie was terrible, a complete waste of time."

sentiment = sentiment_analysis_model(review)[0]

print(sentiment)

# Analyze sentiment analysis results for potential biases in the model itself
```

4. Creative Visionary: Push the Boundaries of Language

- **Dreamer and Doer:** Imagine new applications for LLMs, like generating personalized educational materials or writing poetry in different styles.
- **Innovation Catalyst:** Experiment with LLMs and push them to their creative limits. Imagine using an LLM to brainstorm new product ideas or even compose music.
- **Trailblazer:** Explore the ethical and societal implications of LLMs and contribute to shaping their responsible development. Imagine advocating for fair and inclusive use of LLMs in various fields.

Remember: These are just the starting chords. Stay tuned for the next section, where we'll explore how to find your dream LLM job and turn your skills into reality!

8.2 Finding Your LLM Dream Job: Where the Magic Happens

Got your LLM rockstar skills honed? Now let's turn them into that dream job! Buckle up, because we're about to map your journey to finding the perfect LLM-focused role, complete with real-world examples and even some code snippets to spark your imagination.

1. Explore Diverse Industries: It's Not Just Tech Anymore

LLMs are like chameleons, blending into various industries and creating exciting opportunities. Here's a taste of what's out there:

- **Healthcare Hero:** Imagine developing chatbots that answer patients' questions or using LLMs to analyze medical data for personalized treatment plans. Think building an LLM-powered chatbot that offers mental health support or using an LLM to analyze medical scans for potential diseases.
- **Finance Whiz:** Think writing AI-powered financial reports or using LLMs to detect fraud in transactions. Imagine coding an LLM to generate stock market predictions based on news articles or developing an LLM-powered tool that identifies suspicious financial activity in real-time.

Code Example (simplified):

Python

```python
# This is a simplified example and wouldn't be used for actual financial predictions
from transformers import pipeline

financial_text_processor = pipeline("text-classification", model="finBERT")
```

```
news_article   =   "Company   XYZ   announces
strong quarterly earnings."

sentiment                                    =
financial_text_processor(news_article)[0]

print(sentiment)

# Remember, financial predictions require
complex models and regulations
```

Education Rockstar: Imagine creating personalized learning materials tailored to individual student needs or using LLMs to grade essays and provide feedback. Think building an LLM-powered platform that generates practice math problems based on a student's learning level or developing an LLM that grades essays and offers constructive criticism.

Remember: This is just a starting point! Explore and find the industry that speaks to your passion.

2. Network and Connect: The Power of Community

The LLM community is buzzing with activity. Here are ways to plug in:

- **LLM Conferences & Workshops:** Meet professionals, learn cutting-edge research, and discover job opportunities. Attend events like ACL (Association for Computational Linguistics) or EMNLP (Empirical Methods in Natural Language Processing).
- **Online Forums & Communities:** Discuss applications, share knowledge, and network. Join platforms like the Hugging Face community or forums like Reddit's r/machinelearning.
- **Follow Industry Leaders:** Stay updated, learn from their experiences, and reach out for guidance. Follow people like Yann LeCun (Meta AI) or Emily M. Bender (University of Washington).

Remember: Building your network opens doors and positions you as a well-connected LLM pro.

3. Showcase Your Skills: Don't Hide Your Light!
Time to make your LLM expertise shine:

- **Open-Source Contributions:** Gain experience, demonstrate skills, and collaborate. Contribute to projects like Hugging Face Transformers or Rasa, an open-source chatbot framework.
- **Hackathons & Coding Challenges:** Test your abilities, solve real-world problems, and win recognition (or even jobs!). Participate in events like the Google AI Language Modeling Hackathon or the Amazon Alexa Prize.

- **Build Your Own Project:** Showcase creativity and innovation. Develop a unique LLM application, like a chatbot that writes poems or an LLM-powered language learning app.

Code Example (simplified):

```python
Python
from transformers import pipeline

poetry_generation_model                        =
pipeline("text-generation",
model="my-creative-writing-model")

prompt = "Write a poem about the stars."

generated_poem                                 =
poetry_generation_model(prompt)[0]["genera
ted_text"]

print(generated_poem)

# Remember, this is a basic example.
Explore advanced LLM capabilities for your
project
```

Remember: A strong portfolio showcasing your LLM skills and experience is key to attracting potential employers.

Stay tuned for the next section, where we'll explore the importance of continuous learning and how to stay ahead of the curve in the ever-evolving world of LLMs!

8.3 Lifelong Learning: Fueling Your LLM Rockstar Journey

The LLM landscape is like a never-ending jam session, constantly evolving and demanding you to jam along. But fear not, fellow rockstar! Here's your guide to staying ahead of the curve, complete with real-world examples and even some code snippets to spark your learning journey:

1. Embrace New Technologies: Be a Tech Tastemaker

Think of yourself as a tech trendsetter, always curious about the hottest tunes on the scene. Here are some ways to stay in the groove:

- **Industry Blogs & Research Papers:** Follow blogs like Hugging Face's, Google AI's, or OpenAI's to stay updated on cutting-edge advancements. Dive into research papers like "Attention is All You Need" (Vaswani et al., 2017) to understand the latest transformer-based algorithms.

- **Cutting-edge ML & NLP Methods:** Explore emerging concepts like zero-shot learning (few-shot prompts for diverse tasks) or factual language models (answering questions based on real-world knowledge). Check out projects like LaMDA from Google AI or Jurassic-1 Jumbo from AI21 Labs.

Code Example (simplified):

Python
```
# Experiment with zero-shot learning using
Bard (remember, actual code may vary)
from transformers import pipeline

zero_shot_model                              =
pipeline("zero-shot-classification",
model="bard")

text    =    "This    movie    was    absolutely
hilarious!"
labels    =    ["positive",    "negative",
"neutral"]

prediction    =    zero_shot_model(text,
labels=labels)[0]

print(prediction)
```

```
# Analyze the results and explore other
zero-shot tasks
```

Responsible AI Practices: As LLMs become more powerful, ethical considerations like bias detection and explainability become crucial. Stay informed about tools like Google's Fairness Indicators or the Algorithmic Justice League's resources.

Remember: Learning never stops! Continuously update your knowledge to stay relevant and unlock the full potential of LLMs.

2. Experimentation is Your Jam Session: Don't Be Shy!

Step onto the stage and jam with LLMs! Get your hands dirty and explore their potential:
- **Try Different LLM Platforms:** Each platform has its unique sound. Jam with tools like Bard, GPT-3, or Jurassic-1 Jumbo to discover your favorite. Participate in online communities like the Hugging Face Hub to explore user-created models.
- **Research Projects:** Contribute to projects tackling real-world challenges in healthcare, education, or environmental science. Join platforms like Zooniverse or collaborate with universities or research labs.

- **Build Your Own (if you're feeling adventurous!):** Don't be intimidated! Start with simple experiments like building a chatbot or generating creative text formats. Gradually increase complexity as you gain experience.

Code Example (simplified):

Python
```
# Experiment with different creative text
formats using Bard (remember, actual code
may vary)
from transformers import pipeline

creative_writing_model                    =
pipeline("text-generation", model="bard")

prompt = "Write a haiku about a sunset."

generated_text                            =
creative_writing_model(prompt)[0]["generat
ed_text"]

print(generated_text)

# Explore other creative formats like
poems, scripts, or song lyrics
```

Remember: Experimentation is where innovation happens. Don't be afraid to break the rules and explore uncharted territories!

3. Sharpen Your Soft Skills: The Human Touch Matters

While technical skills are your guitar riffs, soft skills are the soulful vocals that complete the song. Here's how to fine-tune them:

- **Communication:** Explain complex LLM concepts to both technical and non-technical audiences. Imagine explaining how an LLM works to your grandma or presenting your research findings at a conference. Practice clarity, engagement, and adapting your message to your audience.
- **Collaboration:** Teamwork makes the dream work! Learn to collaborate effectively with developers, researchers, and other professionals. Participate in open-source projects or online communities like the LLM Discord server.
- **Critical Thinking:** Analyze LLM outputs with a critical eye. Identify potential biases, question assumptions, and propose solutions to ethical challenges. Don't just accept results blindly; think critically and improve!

Remember: The human element is crucial in the LLM era. Combine your technical skills with strong communication, collaboration, and critical thinking to become a true LLM rockstar.

Stay tuned for the exciting next chapter, where we'll delve into the societal impact of LLMs, exploring their potential to revolutionize our world and the challenges we need to address. Buckle up, the adventure continues!

CONCLUSION

YOUR LLM ROCKSTAR JOURNEY TAKES FLIGHT!

So, fellow explorers, we've reached the end of this whirlwind tour of the LLM universe. But remember, this is just the first chord in your rockstar journey! The stage is set, your skills are honed, and the possibilities are limitless. Now it's time to step into the spotlight and shape the future of data science with LLMs.

A Call to Action: Own Your Power!

LLMs are more than just tech marvels; they're tools with immense potential to transform our world. The question is: how will you use them? Here are some ways to make your mark:

- **Become an Ethical Champion:** As LLMs become more pervasive, ethical considerations like fairness and bias become crucial. Use your skills to advocate for responsible LLM development and mitigate potential harms.
- **Innovate and Experiment:** Don't be afraid to push boundaries and explore uncharted territories. Build your own LLM projects, participate in hackathons, and contribute to open-source initiatives. Let your creativity flow and see what you can achieve!

- **Educate and Collaborate:** Share your knowledge with others, inspire the next generation of LLM rockstars, and collaborate with diverse communities. Remember, together we can achieve much more!

RESOURCES FOR YOUR EXPLORATION: FUELING YOUR LLM ROCKSTAR JOURNEY

Remember, the learning never stops! Here are some valuable resources to keep your LLM flame burning bright:

Online Communities:

- **Forums:**
  o LLM Discord server: Connect with a vibrant community of LLM enthusiasts and experts.
  o Hugging Face community: Engage in discussions, share projects, and learn from fellow Hugging Face users.
  o Reddit's r/machinelearning: Dive into broader machine learning discussions and connect with the larger ML community.

- **Social Media:**
  o Follow industry leaders and researchers on Twitter or LinkedIn to stay updated on the latest developments.
  o Join Facebook groups dedicated to LLMs and related fields
  o .

Research Papers and Blogs:

- **Research Papers:**
  - arXiv: Explore a vast repository of research papers, including many on LLMs and related fields like NLP and machine learning.
  - ACL Anthology: Access research papers presented at leading conferences like the Association for Computational Linguistics.
  - Google AI Blog: Stay updated on cutting-edge research and advancements from Google AI, including LLM-related projects.

- **Industry Blogs:**
  - Hugging Face Blog: Follow the latest developments from the Hugging Face team, including blog posts, tutorials, and project showcases.
  - OpenAI Blog: Get insights into the work of OpenAI, a leading research lab focused on artificial intelligence.
  - Google AI Blog: Read about the latest research and projects from Google AI, including advancements in LLMs.

Open-Source Projects:

- **GitHub:** Explore a vast range of open-source LLM projects, libraries, and tools. Some popular ones include:
  - Transformers: The core library for many LLM models and applications.
  - Bard: Google's open-source language model platform.
  - Jurassic-1 Jumbo: A massive open-sourced LLM model from AI21 Labs.

- **Hugging Face Hub:** Discover and utilize pre-trained LLM models, datasets, and other resources shared by the community.

Additional Resources:

- **Online Courses:** Platforms like Coursera, edX, and Udacity offer courses on various aspects of LLMs and related fields.
- **Workshops and Conferences:** Attend industry events like ACL, EMNLP, or the Google AI Language Modeling Hackathon to learn from experts and network with others.
- **Books and Articles:** Stay informed by reading books and articles about LLMs, their applications, and their impact on society.

Remember, this is just a starting point! Explore other resources, stay curious, and keep learning to continuously push the boundaries of your LLM expertise. The future is yours to shape!

LOOKING AHEAD: THE EVOLVING LLM LANDSCAPE: A GLIMPSE BEYOND THE HORIZON

We've explored the exciting potential of LLMs, honed our skillsets, and are ready to rock the world. But the LLM landscape, like a fast-flowing river, never stands still. So, buckle up, fellow rockstars, as we peer into the swirling currents of the future:

1.   Algorithmic   Advancements: Beyond Transformers?

While transformers currently reign supreme, new architectures and algorithms are bubbling under the surface. Will neuromorphic computing or quantum AI bring about a paradigm shift? Will we see models that learn to reason, understand emotions, or even generate entirely new forms of creative expression? Stay tuned for exciting possibilities!

2. Democratization of LLMs: Power to the People?

Currently, access to large, powerful LLMs is limited to major tech companies or research labs. But what if LLMs became more accessible, like powerful tools available to anyone with an internet connection? Imagine democratizing creative writing, personalized education, or even scientific discovery! However, ethical considerations regarding bias, misuse, and potential job displacement need careful attention.

3. The Societal Impact: A Double-Edged Sword?

LLMs' impact on society will be profound. Imagine AI-powered news articles that shape public opinion, chatbots that provide therapy or legal advice, or even deepfakes so realistic they blur the lines of truth. We must navigate these ethical minefields responsibly, ensuring LLMs augment and empower humanity, not harm or manipulate it.

4. The Human-LLM Symbiosis: Partners, Not Replacements

Fear not, fellow humans! LLMs are not here to replace us. Instead, they offer the potential to become powerful collaborators, amplifying our creativity, problem-solving skills, and knowledge. Imagine the breakthroughs possible when human intuition and LLM capabilities join forces!

5. The Unforeseen: Embracing the Unknown

Predicting the future is a fool's errand, and the LLM landscape is no exception. Unexpected discoveries, technological breakthroughs, and even unforeseen ethical challenges could emerge, shaping the field in unimaginable ways. Stay curious, adaptable, and ready to face the exciting unknown!

This is just a taste of the thrilling journey ahead. Remember, you are not just an observer, but an active participant in shaping the future of LLMs. So, keep learning, keep innovating, and keep rocking! The world awaits your unique contribution to this ever-evolving landscape.